Mud 2 Millions

Ayesha Selden's 7 Step Wealth Cheat Codes

Our Company

In 2019, Adrian Kennedy began publishing books for independent authors from his office in Charlotte, North Carolina. His goal was to provide authors with more options and control over the publishing process at prices anyone could afford.

Today, the family owned and operated, Xscape Publishing company still continues to honor the founder's tradition of providing high-quality products and valuable services to the community.

First published by Xscape Publishing 2020

Copyright © 2020 Ayesha Selden

ISBN 978-1-7351852-3-1

Table of Contents

Introduction:

Why I Love Cheat Codes

When I was a kid, I loved to play my Nintendo. I sat there for hours transfixed in that world of cartoon characters looking for coins and running to a finish line. But, my favorite part of any game was figuring out the cheat codes the programmer buried in the game for the most clever players to find and use to their advantage to beat an opponent.

Those cheat codes gave me an unfair advantage over my enemies and competitors in the game. I leveraged those cheat codes, along with the skill I acquired from hours of practice, and mastered the games. While I stopped playing video games well before my teens, they taught me an invaluable lesson that would work in my favor later in life. In real life, there are various hacks and cheat codes that give us advantages over the system.

The trick is to figure out those codes and apply muscle and work ethic to perfecting the execution of them. I have designed this book as a short and sweet guide to wealth cheat codes. This is your abbreviated manual to exploit the system that was not designed for you to win and have that same system work in your favor. Consider this the Cliffs Notes to your first million.

Let me say up front that this e-book has a very specific audience. This is for the folks who, like me, grew up in poverty and were never given the financial literacy cheat codes to become a millionaire well before normal retirement age.

I am not here to give you a sob story, because I love every step and obstacle of my journey, but I will say I came from nothing. I've got the whole teenage, single mom, come from the hood story that many of you do. No one in my family was wealthy. And my childhood investment knowledge came from watching movies like Trading Places and Wall Street, as a kid in the 80's. And while I couldn't, for the life of me, figure out how concentrated frozen orange juice was making people money, I was certain that if Billy Ray Valentine could figure it out, so could I.

I am second generation college educated and by the time I graduated from Temple University, I had one goal: become a millionaire by 30—which I did shortly after my 30th birthday. This quick read is a hack on how to hit that millionaire mark and it's everything I wish someone would have told me earlier.

If you're a friend trying to elevate your circle, I want you to read this with your squad. If you're a parent wanting better for your bloodline, I want you to read this with your children. If you're a grandchild and gramps still has some spit fire in him, I want you to read this with him. I don't ever want you to think it's too late for greatness. Some of the world's most successful businesses were founded by men and women much later in their lives. If you're already in your 30s, 40s, or 50s+, that's cool, beloved. We are all on different journeys and your wealth building must start somewhere. Let it begin with this knowledge.

I recently posted this 7-step wealth hack on my Twitter and IG pages and got so many messages asking clarifying questions on each of the steps, I wanted to give you all more details on each step. To be clear, steps 1-6 aren't optional if you're building straight from the mud like I did. I will tell you that most of you will try to skip step 2 and fail because it's almost impossible to out-earn poor spending habits. I'll talk more about that in a bit.

Before you dig in, I need you to make a commitment. Commit to yourself that this isn't going to be just another self-help book you scan and walk away with a ton of great ideas that stay just that: ideas.

Commit to getting out of your own head, out of your own way and to EXECUTE.

I'll leave you (and start you!) with this disclaimer: I don't mince words and I'm terrible at sugarcoating. If you've spent any time reading my mini blogs online, you'll know that I won't make a point to deliver the info sweetly—I'll give it to you exactly as it is, beloved. There are some hard, cold truths that we have to face about where we are financially. And honey on shit is still shit, fam.

I will also say that there is no judgement in between these lines. For years, I have given, for free, tons of information on wealth building through social media platforms, podcasts and classes. I do it because I am always rooting for the underserved. I will forever remain a cheerleader for the ones they counted out. I stan for those that came from nothing because that is the story of those I have always loved the most. That is my family. That is me. That is you. (This is feeling like a wealth love letter. K bye.)

Cheers,

Ayesha

Step 1:

Change your mindset about money & eff the Jones' you've been keeping up with.

"Every aspect of your life would hit different if you realized you ain't gotta prove shit to anyone but yourself." @ayeshaselden 10:36 AM ·11/6/19 ·Twitter for iPhone

How we think about money is the genesis and revelation of wealth creation. I'd like you to take a moment to swallow this dose I am about to give. Ask yourself this question:

What is the purpose of the money we make?

While that may seem like a basic question, your answer to it is probably the single greatest catalyst of whether you will defy the odds and become a millionaire or become another US statistic that is woefully unprepared for even a low cost emergency. I want you to really think about that question because I am about to get personal and, for some of you, deliver a bit of a blow.

Do you see money as a bridge to freedom? Or do you see money as a conduit to feed your consumer desires?

I would argue that most people get paid and mostly think of how they're going to spend money to consume.

CHANGE YOUR MINDSET ABOUT MONEY & EFF THE JONES' YOU'VE BEEN KEEPING UP WITH.

I read a tweet recently that said, "a high income with no desire to impress anyone is a potent combination for saving a ridiculous amount of money." I don't know who to credit for that one but there is so much power in those words. We have to ask ourselves why and how we make decisions with our money. What (or who) are we spending for? Does our money serve some purpose? Do we need designer and expensive items for ourselves? Or are we trying to maintain an image of what we believe wealth looks like?

I have been in personal finance for two decades. I get the privilege of sitting down with average Americans and helping them manage and account for their money. Growing up poor in Philadelphia, I had no idea what real wealth looked like before I started my profession as a financial planner. Real money was either in a business suit on TV or a drug dealer driving a nice car around "Saigon", the neighborhood I grew up in. Hood money was flashy and something we aspired to as kids. God help the kids who didn't have the most expensive Jordans or designer clothes. They were endlessly ridiculed and called poor which, in retrospect, was interesting because we all lived in deep poverty. That was the culture.

I got my first crack at learning what real money looked like when I worked as a bank teller in college.

I'll never forget. Shortly after I was hired, a woman walked in the branch in head to toe Gucci and, my 20-year old self, thought: "she is the epitome of money."

I've been curious about affluence my entire life and I hoped I got to wait on this rich lady thinking maybe she would give me a quick nugget on how I could be rich like her. I got my wish and

Ms. Gucci Drip was standing at my window making a cash deposit. I took her deposit slip and about $200 in cash and couldn't wait to see her balance information, which I was sure would be as robust as the diamond on her finger.

I almost fell off of my high chair when I realized that her deposit cleared her negative balance and brought her account up to a positive $87. I looked back at her and thought maybe she has accounts somewhere else and this is just a place she parks money from time to time.

Giving her the benefit of the doubt, I decided to proceed with the upsell training we got as tellers to try push higher end accounts that gave customers better interest rates. I told her that if she has accounts at other places, she could merge them into one of our premier accounts with a $2,500 minimum balance. I watched a woman wearing at least $50,000 worth of jewelry tell me that this was her only account. She had $87 to her name.

Fam.

I found out in my early 20s, as a Stock Broker and Certified Financial Planner, that my wealthiest clients were the ones who, at least from outward appearance, looked the poorest. It completely blew my mind.

They were The Millionaire Next Door in real life. My millionaire clients were not flashy. They drove Hondas, Toyotas and Subaru's for crying out loud. Their clothes were clean and neat but generally not designer items.

Most of their money was spent on saving for emergencies, investing for retirement and educating their children.

CHANGE YOUR MINDSET ABOUT MONEY & EFF THE JONES' YOU'VE BEEN KEEPING UP WITH.

Discretionary expenses like trips were planned in advance and budgeted. They were nothing at all like what I thought wealth was and yet they had millions. I asked them questions and I listened to them. I emulated their habits. I refused to spend frivolously. I had a plan.

So, I learned from experience as a bank teller and financial planner, all that glitters ain't gold. And the poor-looking millionaires were using the cheat codes to wealth.

Let's talk about the most important cheat code, spending less than you make. This one code will keep you safe through thick and thin.

Step 2:

Cut Expenses and Make Sacrifices.

"Every man is a consumer, and ought to be a producer. He is by constitution expensive, and needs to be rich." – Ralph Waldo Emerson

For most folk, delayed gratification, which is putting off what we currently want most for something greater in the future, is a deal breaker. Most, I believe, are stuck at the conflicting intersection of having the desire to be wealthy but unwilling to sacrifice short term. And this contention, along with lack of knowledge, puts us on the struggle bus of falling victim to get- rich-quick schemes and why millions of us throw our hard-earned money at the lottery when you've legit got a better chance of being struck by lightening. True story.

Many of you are vexed by and get defensive at just hearing the word "sacrifice" but this is the most crucial step toward building your first million. The word sacrifice means 'to make sacred'. A sacrifice signifies that you take something that you used to think was less important and make it more important in your life. People used to sacrifice animals to signify that God was more important than the food, money, or gifts they sacrificed.

Here, when you sacrifice, you are saying that what you need to make you a millionaire is more important than what you want that makes you poor. You get to choose between spending $15 at Qdoba or $15 to save and invest so you have more than $15 in the future. To go from mud to millions, you have to choose your future wealth and prosperity consistently and over and over and over.

Now let's dispel a quick myth. Many genuinely believe that if they make more money, their money problems go away. That is fake news. Let me be the first to tell you that it is almost impossible to out-earn poor spending habits. Read that last sentence again. Many of you will take pause to me saying that but allow me to prove to you why I am correct with some statistics.

A 2018 CNBC article reported that an estimated 60% of NBA players go broke within 5 years of retiring. If that's not bad enough, approximately 78% of NFL players experience financial hardship within just two years of retirement.

While we've heard countless stories of lottery winners who end up broke, the most classic is of William Post III who won a $16.2 million lottery in 1988. Within 3 months, Post was $500k in debt. By the end of his life, he was over $1 million in debt.

If you don't learn how to effectively manage your finances when you're making $2,000 a month, you'll still struggle when you're making $20,000 a month because your lifestyle expenses will rise at the same or faster rate than your income. This is known as lifestyle inflation.

We increase our expenses, as our income rises. It's almost a natural progression as we mentally rationalize what we deserve and what we may subconsciously need to prove to others as a barometer of our success. I'm a fan of flaunting it, but only after you're actually wealthy (see Step 7).

If you practice lifestyle inflation, you will be no better off financially when you earn a higher salary. You may have better stuff, but you'll still use poor spending habits.

I know plenty of high income earners that can't save money. And let me assure you that there are people who make significantly less than high income earners and can pay their bills and still have money left over for saving & investing. The difference is fully accounting for your income and budgeting your discretionary spending.

Here's a visual illustration of what lifestyle inflation looks like:

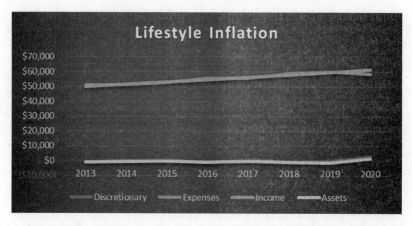

You'll see that over the seven years, this person keeps spending as much as they earn. As their income increases, they generally upgrade their cars and/or living space. You'll also notice that the blue line, discretionary income (money left over after paying your committed expenses like mortgage or rent, utilities, car payments etc.), is sometimes negative. This shows what happens when you use credit, you owe more in bills than you have income.

I am not suggesting that your lifestyle never increase with your income. We should reward ourselves for all the hard work we put in. But why do we feel as if we "deserve" to inflate or increase how much we spend at the same rate as our income?

Does a wage increase require a newer car, or a new-to-us car? Does a bonus mean we have to upgrade our homes? By all means, fix what's broken. But increasing our lifestyle at a vastly slower rate than our income rewards us with the ultimate payoff: freedom.

Here's a better alternative to the visual illustration above:

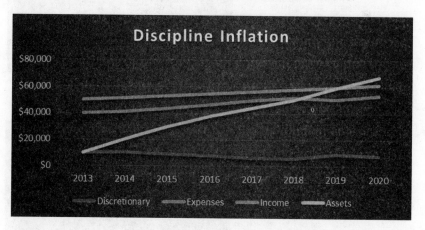

There's an alternative to lifestyle inflation, which keeps you teetering on poverty. I call it discipline inflation. Discipline inflation means you choose to save and invest more and more of your money over time. This isn't for the faint of heart.

Now, let's compare lifestyle inflation (bad) with discipline inflation (good). The thing to keep your eye on in the table is the impact of lifestyle and discipline inflation on your assets (yellow line). With lifestyle inflation, you end up reducing your assets by

$2,505. If you didn't have any funds in savings, you've transferred that $2,505 onto credit cards which then requires you to pay interest on your spending habits. Conversely, with discipline inflation, you've increased your assets by over $67,000. With discipline inflation, you'll save more and become worth more money over time, as represented by the yellow asset line.

I'm also putting in the tables of numbers because at some time, you'll have to deal with numbers as you amass your fortune.

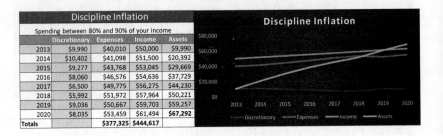

Lifestyle Inflation

Spending between 95% and 105% (credit!) of your income

	Discretionary	Expenses	Income	Assets
2013	($800)	$50,800	$50,000	($800)
2014	$210	$51,290	$51,500	($590)
2015	($2,827)	$55,872	$53,045	($3,417)
2016	($926)	$55,562	$54,636	($4,343)
2017	$729	$55,546	$56,275	($3,613)
2018	($1,907)	$59,871	$57,964	($5,521)
2019	($268)	$59,971	$59,703	($5,789)
2020	$3,284	$58,210	$61,494	($2,505)
Totals		$447,122	$444,617	

Discipline Inflation

Spending between 80% and 90% of your income

	Discretionary	Expenses	Income	Assets
2013	$9,990	$40,010	$50,000	$9,990
2014	$10,402	$41,098	$51,500	$20,392
2015	$9,277	$43,768	$53,045	$29,669
2016	$8,060	$46,576	$54,636	$37,729
2017	$6,500	$49,775	$56,275	$44,230
2018	$5,992	$51,972	$57,964	$50,221
2019	$9,036	$50,667	$59,703	$59,257
2020	$8,035	$53,459	$61,494	$67,292
Totals		$377,325	$444,617	

With discipline inflation, meaning the ability to make small sacrifices over time, your expenses aren't escalating at the same pace as your income. As a result of executing this discipline over time, your savings continue to rise and eventually your assets exceed your annual income. By effectively learning how to invest those savings, your assets eventually become a large multiple of your annual income (20 times or greater). We will talk about investing in a later chapter. You'll also notice that with discipline inflation, your spending does increase, but never exceeds 90% of your income. The inflation means that as you earn more, you save more.

There are many reasons the people fall into lifestyle inflation. The most obvious is that we were never taught to be disciplined with our money. The other is that commercials have trained us to believe in a pathological consumerism: overcompensating for childhood lack, filling voids with stuff, the need to put up appearances so that others think you're doing better than you actually are. The long-term ramification of commercials, consumerism and lifestyle inflation devastates our wealth building, and that has an impact for generations.

You ever notice that there are no commercials for not spending money? You won't find anyone advertising that you should shop at Wal-mart instead of Target and invest the money you save. There's no soothing music when you're making hard decisions not to go to the Chinese store or fast food joint and eat your rice and beans you think you're too tired to cook at home. As Gil Scott Heron said, the revolution will not be televised.

The excuse I hear most often, against sacrificing what you want for what you need by cutting expenses, is generally something like: "tomorrow isn't promised so we need to live for today." It always especially startles me when I hear parents say things like this because their current finances clearly indicate that they believe tomorrow is promised.

They typically lack enough savings, assets or insurance to even put them in the ground, let alone leave a legacy. These same people will rail on about how they could be gone tomorrow so they might as well get those shoes they want today. Most either don't know or don't care about the ramifications of heavy consumerism. To put it bluntly, because you decided to splurge while alive, it's up to your family to kill every blue fish in the state just to fry and sell enough platters to put you in the ground? These decisions to inflate your lifestyle, at the same rate as your income, are not based in logic—it is rationalizing to get what you want.

Another form of rationalized spending that I hear quite often: "I don't spend a lot but I still have no money left over." I'd encourage you to do this exercise below:

CASH FLOW RECON MISSION:

1) Gather your bank and credit card statements **for the last 90 days**. If you get them electronically, print them out (at the library if you need to) or call your bank to send you a new copy.

2) Go down each statement line item by line item and put a star next to or use a highlighter to highlight any purchases or ATM withdrawals that were "wants" and not "needs". This includes: ordering out, entertainment, cable TV, cigarettes, liquor or marijuana (not for real medical use), buying lunch every day, brand name clothes, bags, and shoes, ATM fees, late charges, subscriptions you don't use, morning lattes, etc.

3) Tally, that's bank teller talk for add up, your highlighted "wants" on all the statements by adding them together.

4) Once you have the total, divide that number by 3 (assuming you pulled 90 days of statement activity). That is the amount of additional money that, on a monthly basis, you are not utilizing to its full potential. I believe our dollars are like soldiers; the goal is to send those dollars out to work hard for you now so that you can work less in the future.

Once you've identified your average monthly underutilized money, make a decision to take at least ½ of that number to get you to that first million. If you're in that rare group of people where there's nothing highlighted and you're still struggling to make ends meet, see me in the next chapter beloved. We've got some income increase work to do stat.

There are some that want a slow and steady climb to the million. For those folk, following Step 2 and subsequently investing that "found money" or "discretionary income" (which I'll talk about in a later chapter) into index funds inside of an IRA or 401(k) over a 30+ year period has created legions of what I call lazy millionaires. I call them lazy because most of them did nothing but direct 10% to 20% of their paycheck into a company retirement plan and maybe occasionally check the value over the years but remain relatively uninvolved in how any of their investments operate. Most of them have all of their money in mutual funds and couldn't even break down how a mutual fund works.

As a real estate investor, I especially call them lazy millionaires because they never have to worry about things like tenant issues, rental maintenance problems, evictions or squatters rights. Most of them have been saving into their company retirement plans for so long, they genuinely forget about the money coming out of their paychecks. They are often shocked to see a seven figure balance in their account as they near their 60s. Here's an example of how this happens:

Lazy Investor Example: Eric

Age: 32

Salary: $55,000/year

Eric's 401(k) contribution: 10%

+ Company Match: 5%

Total Contribution: 15%

Annual $ Contribution: $8,250 (15% of $55k)

Example average return: 8%

Lazy Eric's retirement plan at age 65: $1.2 million

# of times Eric even voted when asked by mutual funds: 0

I'm not mad at Eric. Because while Eric did nothing but sit at home and watch tv every night, he executed quite flawlessly what most Americans can't do: commit 10% of his income to an account he wouldn't touch until retirement. I've read studies that suggest the average 65 year old has less than $65,000 total saved for retirement. How are we feeling about lazy Eric now?

So, what you should do is calculate how much money you spend on the little things every month. Go open an IRA or Roth IRA or 401K account and, every month, put half of that amount in that retirement account. (Consult a tax advisor or financial professional to determine what would be best for you).

I hate when stores tell you that you're going to 'save money'. Technically, you're saving money on what you're buying from them, but then you go and spend that money somewhere else. They don't like to remind you of that. So you should ignore how much money you 'save' and start paying attention to how much money you 1. Spend and 2. Invest.

Next, we're going to look at ways you can earn more money, so that you can put more money into your investments or flip into making more money on bigger projects with better clients.

Step 3:

Generate Additional Income Through a Business or Side Hustle.

*"The dream is free. The hustle is sold separately." –
Unknown*

There are some of you that look at Eric's story and think one of two things: 1) You don't have the patience to wait 33 years to become a millionaire. In the words of the young, legendary urban poet, better known as Drake, "F*** being rich when I'm forty, man, I'm tryna make it now." 2) You may already be in your 40s or 50s and have no intention of working until your 70s or 80s to become a millionaire.

If you're in either of those two boats, this is your chapter. This chapter is also especially a hack for the folks that look at their monthly budgets and genuinely have no opportunity to cut any expenses and still find themselves living paycheck to paycheck.

In the year of our Lord 2020, you can pick your poison (or passion) as a side business. In the vastness of Beyonce's internet, your additional household income is just waiting for you to stop binge-watching Netflix murder mysteries and dedicate time to something that will help you build a legacy.

Some of the most popular side hustles I see (in no particular order) are:

GENERATE ADDITIONAL INCOME THROUGH A BUSINESS OR SIDE HUSTLE.

a. Wholesaling real estate: An unlicensed individual getting a contract to buy a house from a seller with the intention of almost immediately selling that contract or property to an end buyer at a higher price. The wholesaler pockets the difference which is often called an assignment fee. I've seen wholesalers make assignment fees as little as $1,000 and as high as six figures.

b. Investing in real estate: Raising capital through flips, buying and selling appreciated lots or generating monthly cash flow through long-term buy and hold rentals. These are just a few of the ways that you can invest in real estate. I could write an entire book on this alone.

c. Becoming a licensed realtor: In many states, wholesaling is now becoming illegal since there is little to no regulation in wholesaling. As a result, I've seen many wholesalers getting a realtor's licensed and selling homes on nights and weekends for commission income.

d. Becoming a general contractor: There is a shortage of skilled tradesman in the US. As real estate investors try to build their portfolios, there's been a surge in the need for reputable contractors. GC's typically hire subcontractors (i. e. plumbers, carpenters, electricians) that typically do the hands on work. The investor or homeowner then pays the GC a fee on top of the price from the subcontractors. That mark-up fee can pay the GC very well.

e. Ride share: Uber/Lyft driving early mornings, nights & weekends. While I think it's virtually impossible to make money doing this when you're leasing the vehicle directly from Uber or Lyft, since the monthly lease price from Uber/Lyft is backbreaking, if you have your own vehicle, you can earn as little as a few hundred to as much as a few extra thousand per month as a ride share operator.

f. Flipping or selling products online: Through companies like Ebay, Etsy and Amazon, folks are making a killing through either original product creation or product arbitrage—finding goods slightly below market prices and then sell them online for a profit. Given the right volume, this can be extremely profitable.

g. Become a virtual assistant: With the rise of the small business entrepreneur, and the need to delegate administrative support or cold calling, virtual assistants get the opportunity to work remotely and earn an attractive income. You can work exclusively for one person or multiple people at once depending on the need, pay and amount of time you have available.

h. Content creating: You have undoubtedly seen the surge of social media content. Blogs, Youtube, online courses, and ebooks have completely changed the entrepreneur landscape. There are video bloggers who get paid six figures for posting highly viewed content via their YouTube channels. In the first 30 days of selling tickets for my very first class, a partner and I raked in approximately $25k with the event still months out. My mind was entirely blown.

i. Multi-Level-Marketing: While I don't personally know anyone that has made the millions generally promised from MLM leaders, there are many who generate additional monthly income through some of the popular companies out there. I recently had dinner with a guy who was an exec in a large MLM years ago. He said he has been disengaged from the org for years but still gets

GENERATE ADDITIONAL INCOME THROUGH A
BUSINESS OR SIDE HUSTLE.

residual income checks of approximately $3k per month from the pyramid structure he built years ago (*insert 'That ain't no problem' Shannon Sharpe . gif here*)

j. Day trading: While I think this is a fairly risky way to earn short-term income, traders have demonstrated that in certain markets they can generate additional income through active trading of stocks, options, digital currency or other assets on an exchange that brings buyers and sellers together. The beauty of this type of income is that it can be done anywhere in the world as long as you have a device that can access the internet. I will say that day trading is not all sweet, however. It still requires some knowledge of the markets you're trading and even the most savvy investors get burned in short-term trades if the market shifts quickly.

k. Offering consulting services: This is a very popular income generation strategy for folks that have demonstrated a competency in a particular field. If you have advanced knowledge in any area, there are individuals willing to pay for your intellectual capital. On Jan 15, 2020 I started offering consults on real estate info I'd been giving away for years. In a little over 30 days, I made $8k without doing much marketing outside of posting the booking link on my IG and Twitter timelines.

l. Getting a second W-2 job: My big sister is a police detective. After working on the force for over a decade, she decided that she wanted to go back to college for a degree in Nursing. She completed a BSN and works some nights and weekends as an RN earning a nice amount of extra monthly cash flow. I told her, in no uncertain terms, the extra cash from the side gig is the net worth building money.

m. Beauty product sales: I've seen everything in this space from local stores that carry hair and beauty product inventory to buying direct from an overseas distributor (or making them yourself) for online sale. This could include hair bundles, wigs, make up, etc.

n. Credit repair businesses: If you follow wealth or real estate social media pages, you will see a credit repair plug. Entrepreneurs are marketing the ability to help people restore their credit and adding to their discretionary income in the process.

o. Vending machines: At a relatively low cost of entry, investors can make solid returns by marketing vending machines to businesses, schools, hospitals, apartment complexes, hotels etc. I've heard of investors buying vending machines for as little as $1,500. The key is good location, products, pricing and keeping up with inventory.

p. Trucking business: There are entrepreneurs that own fleets of trucks and make great money with low involvement in the business. With proper delegation of truck driver hires and product transporting dispatchers, you can manage this entire business from the comforts of your own home.

The quote at the beginning of this chapter tells you that the hustle is sold separately. I'm not about to give you a litany of resources that you could just google while you're watching Netflix. You have to research these different topics and choose which ones are right for you.

Nobody said it will be easy or quick. Better believe that you're going to spend 100 hours trying to figure out how to learn about, set up and start making money in any of these businesses. It may take less, it will probably take more than 100 hours. I just want you to know that if you keep at it, all that hard work will quite literally pay off. And when it does, you can take me to lunch in another country. TYVM

Suffice it to say, there's a variety of options. Your responsibility is to choose and execute.

Step 4:

Save the Difference Between Your Income & Expenses.

Discretionary Income Builds Your Net Worth .

"Making extra income is cool. Cutting unneeded expenses is great. Doing both simultaneously while Stacking/investing the difference births GREATNESS." @ayeshaselden 12:55 PM ·1/3/2020 ·Twitter for iPhone

In Step 2, I discussed reducing expenses. In Step 3, I discussed ways that you can generate additional income. Step 2 alone, cutting expenses and investing the difference, can make you wealthy over time. Step 3, increasing income through a side hustle and investing the extra income, can do the same.

The most efficient and powerful way to expedite wealth, is doing both: cutting expenses and increasing income, at the same damn time. When you:

1. reduce your expenses,

2. practice discipline inflation,

3. supplement your salary with side hustle income,

4. and invest the additional discretionary income,

you will get to your first million in lightning speed.

That's the drink, now here's the chaser: if you want to hit the mark even faster, use any gains or income (that comes from your investments) to reinvest back into either the asset that generated the income or another investment. (I'll talk about reinvesting in Chapter 6.) But first things first: before you can become a great investor, you need to first learn to save. And before you can learn to save, you need to become fully self-aware of your relationship with money.

If you've read this far along, you deserve the real life hack I am about to give you. Folks have asked the secret to going from being a black girl raised by a single mom in the hood of South Philly to becoming a millionaire by 30. I'm about to unleash how that fully came to fruition over the next two chapters.

While I don't intend for this book to be an autobiography, I'd like to give a little background context on how I became a saver and then forged myself into an investor. From the outside looking in, most would argue that I had a disadvantaged upbringing— coming along in the era of Philadelphia's crack epidemic in the late '70s to a teen mom with no present father. I know my father's name is David Williams but couldn't tell you, to this day, if that man is dead or alive. But I had one advantage that this bird's eye view doesn't tell: Mom.

Standing squarely at 4 feet and 11 proud inches, young Cheryl Selden had all the energy and all the smoke of 10 tall mothers. She had an impossible reach. She loved me fiercely. She raised me Philly tough. She surrounded me with a village of strong, independent women that were her friends. She taught me to be fair. She taught me not to let anyone bully me—so I fought a lot. She taught me to trust God. I fought some more when he didn't show up.

I watched this tiny woman put my bikes together and run the household. I learned to listen to my intuition. I fell in love with words because I was forced, not asked, to turn the television off and read books my mom assigned to my sister and I—in addition to our school reading. I didn't think there was a thing in the world a woman couldn't do.

I have argued for years that I am self-made but a wiser me realizes there are flaws in this argument. The fierce love and stern guidance of which I was the unmerited benefactor gave me more than a silver spoon ever could have. If there is a such thing as love privilege, I got it. Fight me.

While my mom was not well educated in the world of investing, she invested heavily in the emotional, spiritual and academic development of her children. She was particularly invested in making sure that my sister and I both loved and feared God. To that end, her plans to solidify my salvation landed me, at 14, in a five-day Christian camp which ended up teaching me an invaluable lesson about people and their money.

On a hot summer Monday in the early 90's, my mom sent me on a "Teens for Jesus" summit down south. She and a friend had arranged for both of their daughters to have a summer revival in that critical year between middle school and high school so that we could start our freshman years filled with the Holy Ghost.

While I was more or less indifferent about the revival part, I was thrilled at being handed $200 for "spending" money. We were staying in a hotel and our accommodations were prepaid. Any money we were given by our parents was intended to cover food and souvenirs. We were given complete and total discretion on our spending and it was each of our responsibility to budget our own money. Mom didn't give me any speeches on how to manage the $200 she gave me. She palmed me ten $20 bills and kissed me goodbye. I felt very grown up.

Our bus rolled out at the crack of dawn on a Monday morning. My friend sat next to me counting her money. Our conference was Monday to Friday and, in her estimation, she would evenly divide her money for each day. She made five stacks of money with $40 in each stack and her plan was simple. She could spend $40 each day to ensure that she wouldn't run out of money until the day we headed home. She beamed with pride in her craftiness to devise such a good plan. While my plan was entirely different, I thought hers was fine enough and stared ahead as we drove into the darkness.

There were mostly black children at the camp. We were all given the same financial charge by our parents, essentially no advice, and I assume we all started out with roughly the same amount of money. I don't remember a thing about what was taught that first day of the conference. I don't remember if I was slain by the Holy Spirit. I do, however, remember the boy we all had to bail out.

At the end of the first day, one of the ministers asked us to form a circle. The minister rested her hands on the shoulders of a small boy and she took him to the middle of our circle. She announced to us that he needed an act of mercy and kindness. This little boy, who we can call Merrill Lynch, had spent all of his money the first afternoon of the conference. The very first mf afternoon. He was broke.

Since there were four days left of the conference, the minister was asking that we all pitch in some money so that he could eat for the rest of the week. I was appalled. I was still sitting pretty with $195 left in my pocket. I'd spent only $5 that day on fast food which had carried me through the day. I remember wondering how in the hell Merrill Lynch had managed to spend all of his money already. And I was pissed at the idea of having to give him any of my money. The minister noticed hesitation from us and asked, in true Christian form, "What Would Jesus Do?" Not spent all his damn money on day one was the only answer I could come up with. The twenty or so of us all came forward and handed him varying bills. I stared hard at a $5 bill and walked up to give it to him. I palmed him the $5 and stared him dead in the eye. I was devastated and I was angry. I believe, at that moment, I may have been America's only black child republican. Down to $190 and four days to go.

Over the next four days of the conference, I tightened my spending belt even further. Young Merrill was an example to me of what not to be. What annoyed me most was that he didn't even appear to be embarrassed about his poor decisions. I glared at him every time he ran into the gift shop thinking this mf got some nerve. TUH! He could barely breathe without me thinking he was off somewhere spending my $5.

I was up in arms over the fact that this idiot had to be bailed out because he couldn't control his spending. I was convinced he would spend the second lot we gave him and was determined not to rescue him again. Not my circus, not my monkey. I tried to forget he existed.

My girlfriend Q, that I traveled with, was doing a wonderful job at sticking to her $40/day spending budget. She would drag me around to the shops on the first floor of the hotel and point out refrigerator magnets, tee shirts and shot glasses that she was buying for everyone back at home. She walked over to me with a glass baby bird and told me I should buy it as a gift. I told her my mom didn't even like birds. I didn't buy one souvenir.

On our final day of the conference, we left in the late afternoon. Q spent her last dollar at a rest stop about 30 miles from home. She was so proud of how she'd managed her money. I kept quiet and stared out the window—anxious to get home. The minute I walked into my bedroom, I managed to slide $175 of the $200 mom sent me away with into a shoe box under my bed. No one got a magnet. No one got a Teen Summit Holy Spirit conference mug. This is still my entire mood.

That trip was a perfect demonstration to 14 year-old me of how differently we all view money. While I hope Merrill Lynch learned how to better budget along the way, I can't say he's very different than many adults today.

The grown version of kid Merrill is the financial disaster of Step 1—attempting to keep up with the Jones'. Buying impulsively, maxing credit cards on designer items, driving a flashy car that they can barely afford to put new brakes on and filing for bankruptcy to clean up the mess. Are there other circumstances that can lead to bankruptcy? Sure. Bad business deals and failing health can cause financial ruin. I am not speaking of unpreventable circumstances that are out of our control. I am referring specifically to the behaviors of those that fall into this category in an attempt to keep up with the Jones' and fall flat on their faces.

They may even be the people who seem the *be* the Jones' until the sun rises on a quiet morning and all the neighbors are shocked to find that the Jones' have packed up and snuck out of their homes, like thieves in the night, before Wells Fargo plants a foreclosure notice on their door. I was grateful to have come face to face with this behavior at 14 and recognized it as a problem.

I believe my friend Q's money "plan" is how most adults manage their household finances. Her goal, which she executed flawlessly, was to figure out how she could run out of money precisely as we got home. This financial stagnation is commonly known as living paycheck to paycheck. If our bus broke down on the way home or severe weather hit and we had to stay an additional day, Q's entire plan would have been stumped.

Millions of adults, literally spend their entire paychecks and go broke the day before pay day without regard to the various emergencies that can arise.

And then there was me. The saver. Maintaining a healthy savings account is a habit that should be taught at an early age. Saving is the first discipline of wealth building. It is the principle behind the notion of paying yourself first. In the first few chapters, we discussed reducing expenses and ways to generate additional income.

The very first step in building wealth comes from piling that discretionary income into 3 to 6 months of your monthly bills as an emergency reserve. If there was anything The Rona has taught us is that our financial responsibility to ourselves is to save up 3-6 months of our expenses just in case. And in this case, it isn't getting fired on our day off, it's a global pandemic. Whatever the reason, you have to sock away 3-6 months of your bills. That's more important than everything except your mortgage and utilities. Once you nail that, you're ready to move onto the next phase of wealth building—investing.

No one had to teach me to save. I was the antithesis of a spender and probably a borderline money hoarder. Anyone earning money should be saving. Parents who pay their children an allowance should teach their child to set aside no less than 10% of their money. The ideal would be some form of bank account where they can track their balance. They should take their kids to the physical bank to deposit the money weekly to get our kids in the habit of saving money.

Even as a kid, I was a financial saver. Saving is innate in me. No one in my family had to or did teach me to save. It was something I just knew to do. I accumulated so much money in the shoebox under my bed, my mom eventually decided to open a passbook savings account for me at PSFS Bank. When I am paid, I always think of myself first, as you should too.

How much of this am I going to keep? I can then part with everything else—often reluctantly. I have had to learn over the years to be a giver. By nature, I am a cheap bastard. I'm not even going to hold you. I hate parting with my money. I felt the vibe of Scrooge McDuck swimming in his vault of money with every fiber of my adolescent being.

Very few adults have committed to the long-term discipline of paying themselves first. In many cases, because of improper budgeting and because we are brainwashed into consumerism, instead of learning the progression of saving to investing, our expenses often exceed our income.

We get our discretionary income and choose not to move wisely. We spend it on wants instead of needs (like stacking 3-6 months of bill money). And when we are broke, the only part of the equation that we focus on is how we aren't paid enough for our hard work. Many argue that they need to make more money. In many cases, I disagree. Many people will be better served paying more attention to how you spend money.

Failure to learn to live below your means will be a problem regardless of how much you make. I have sat down with dual income households that earn in excess of a half a million dollars per year and couldn't save $300 per month if their life depended on it. People often think increased income will teach them how to be better stewards of their finances. The best time to learn how to manage your funds is when the stakes are lower.

The ability to live below our means and reconcile our budgets (income minus expenses) reproduces the ability to set aside the difference. This is called savings. The ability to not touch those funds for wants takes an incredible amount of discipline. That discipline is what will make or break your journey to your first million.

While I was a natural born saver, it took me a while to realize that being a saver wasn't a destination in itself. It would take more than just being a saver to become a millionaire. There are only 24 hours a day and I'm only working 8 to 12 of them. I needed to figure out how my savings could work for me while I worked **and** while I slept. That is the destination. That is investing.

Step 5:

Learn how to invest the difference.

"The stock market is a device to transfer money from the impatient to the patient." – Warren Buffett

The late '90s were the dawn of the internet revolution. Tech and dotcom firms exploded with unprecedented growth and I wanted to double or triple my money. My first investment was a technology mutual fund. Like everyone else in the late 90s, I was driven by greed because dotcom companies were seeing unprecedented gains.

I bought a tech fund because everyone boasted their high returns. Within two years, I'd lost about 70% of my principal investment.

I was devastated, at the time, but it's the best thing that could have happened. It was a lesson I needed and would begin guiding and developing disciplines I would learn later. I had not yet heard of the legendary financial genius Warren Buffett who warns investors to be "fearful when others are greedy and greedy when others are fearful". I was still a rookie and an undisciplined investor who thought the markets were sweet and that money was fast. I would learn, with this investment, (and others in subsequent years where my greed got the best of me) that there are no easy short cuts to wealth. These lessons taught me that most would-be investors' instinct is to chase money based on emotions and not technical expertise, market fundamentals or even logic. Most people literally approach investment markets with the exact same strategies that they use when pulling a chair up to a blackjack table in Las Vegas. You probably think I'm blowing smoke but let me give you some stats.

A 2017 study comparing the 30-year average annual return of the US stock market versus the actual returns for the average investor illustrates a staggering performance gap. While the S&P 500 returned a 10.16% average return, individuals who invested in the US stock market, over the same time frame, saw a return of only 3.98%.

Why did the average investor underperform the market by such a significant spread? Emotional investing. Emotional investors will sell a stock on the first inkling of a downturn, and buy a stock after it's already gone up. Fear of market losses will often have an investor selling a stock at a price, and they won't buy it again until it goes back up to that price or even exceeds it. If the stock was a quality company:

a. you probably shouldn't have sold it in the first place and

b. you're now buying it when it's more expensive.

If I were to ask you, how do you make money in a market, your response would be something like "buy it low and sell it high." And although we could argue that there are more factors in that equation, like receiving dividend or rental income from that investment, buy low/sell high would be a fairly accurate statement.

To put it simply, the goal of an investor is generally to buy an asset at or below market price and to sell it for a higher price in the future. While that sounds great in theory, there is a study called Behavioral Finance that indicates that we, far too often, allow our emotions to govern when we buy and when we sell.

Financial strategy aside, decisions tend to look more like this: when an investment drops 30%, no one wants it and people who already own it want to sell it because their fears kick into overdrive and they start to imagine losing everything. When an investment increases 30%, however, people want to buy it. The driving factors are fear of losing and the greed of possibility of what has already happened.

I would argue that FOMO (fear of missing out) governs most buy/sell behaviors. There is the fear of missing out on gains in an up market and fear of keeping your money in a down market. I wish I could say that poor investment I made in the tech fund in '99 would be my last one. It took me a couple of years of getting burned to learn to avoid chasing returns and make disciplined and hard decisions with my investments.

Let me tell you about how I went from a financially uneducated, cheap bastard to becoming a multi-millionaire investor.

I am second-generation college educated. With the motivation of having kids at age 16 & 19, my mom put herself through nursing school and then worked as a nurse at Temple Hospital for most of my life. A single income with two kids still kept us poor, and in the hood, but we had luxuries, like a car, an in-house washer & dryer, that most of our neighbors didn't have.

Mom's job was also the plug because my full $20,000 college tuition was paid for mostly because she was an employee of Temple Hospital and partially because I worked full time at a bank while in college (and my job picked up the cost of the summer classes that mom's job didn't pay for). To avoid going into any debt for college, I decided to scrap my "A Different World" fantasies of living on campus (which was not covered) and stayed at home and commuted to school every day in the '88 Chevy Beretta I saved to buy working at McDonalds from age 16 to 18.

I paid for my first semester of books with money I earned working and by my second semester, I had a hustle of selling my former semester books to lower classmates so that I could use that money to pay for my next semester's books. It is also not lost on me that most universities today aren't as cheap as Temple was in '96 when I attended. Even TU, which didn't have a great reputation when I enrolled, has become more prestigious and has more than tripled in price since my freshman year—24 years ago. I remember at 17, wanting to attend University of Southern California but, even as a teenager, I was not interested in borrowing that kind of money for school.

My majors in college were Economics and Marketing but, even in the school of business, I didn't take any classes that provided mastery on managing personal finances. Working as a bank teller outside of class hours and servicing customers with high cash and mutual fund accounts is where I really got interested in investing.

A week after I graduated from college, I flew with friends to the island of Freeport in the Bahamas. I knew it was going to be my last hoorah before starting the grind of my 20s. Three weeks later, I started a job in Conshohocken, PA in personal finance with a big, blue-chip company and, in a couple of years, I finally put the pieces of the puzzle together to hit my wealth building stride.

Most of us are taught growing up that it isn't polite to talk to strangers about money. This took some personal growth because by October 18, 2000, talking to strangers about money was what I was fully licensed, appointed and being paid to do. I also found that my white counterparts were more comfortable talking about money than the few minorities that started my financial planning career with me.

I'll never forget how embarrassed I got when a 5'3 dark haired guy came into a group meeting and introduced himself as LP, our Group Vice President, and before he even asked our names, he turned on an overhead projector and put up a slide of his personal investment account statement, that showed us all his millions.

Almost every movie about Wall Street and investing has a scene like this.

Everyone in the room was young and hungry. We were all working at least 60-80 hours/week and making about $30,000 a year at best. LP was probably in his late 40s at the time and told us that the overhead we were gawking at wasn't even the bulk of his wealth. He said most of his money was in real estate assets he and his wife had been buying in Boston over the years. I looked around the room and all eyes were on that overhead screen. LP was an entire mood.

Over the next year, I had the privilege of working for and learning from LP. He was a US Navy pilot turned financial professional so his mandatory personal development classes I attended were dripping with lessons in self-mastery, personal accountability, emotional intelligence and work ethic.

It was the Mamba mentality from a short Jewish guy and a second coming of age for me. It was like white collar bootcamp lol. I think I may have yelled, "YES DRILL SERGEANT!" in at least a dozen classes.

LP talked incessantly about not overthinking things. I'll never forget the sting he gave the analytic in me when he said, "when you think, you weaken the nation". His point was that overthinking causes lack of action. And lack of action stifles results and success. Results and success put capital back into the economy and overthinking combats that.

Larry told us to outwork everyone around us and privately told me that, as a black woman, I needed to outwork all the white guys around me. He wasn't lying.

The summer I started with my firm, there were at least 100 of us hired—mostly guys that were recent college grads. LP was widely respected but not very well liked because he had zero tolerance for excuses and would embarrass you if your productivity numbers were low. He would call on you in a class of about 100 folks and tell you to sell him something. We had scripts, at the time, and if you didn't recite the script verbatim, from memory, he would make you look like an idiot. I took what LP said as a roadmap to my success. When everyone went home, I would stay for hours after work to know my scripts cold. If everyone else in the room made 500 calls, I would stay later and make 1000. "Rumble young man, rumble."

One of the most eye-opening things I learned working in personal finance is that most of the professionals giving advice (stockbrokers, insurance agents and investment advisors) are broke because they don't practice what they preach. LP told us to save and invest no less than 20% of our income as rookies so that when our incomes soared, we would be in the habit already. Paying myself before anything or anyone became a principal I began to live by.

He also told us if we listened to his self-mastery principals that we'd make a ton of money but to never forget that our first financial obligation was to secure our own masks first. Airplanes are equipped with oxygen masks in case a door pops off or a window breaks. At 20,000 feet there isn't much air, so you need the extra oxygen. At the beginning of every flight, the flight attendants instruct you to put on your own mask first if there's an emergency. You're no help to anyone if you pass out before you can put your mask on your family, friends, and seatmates.

Putting on my own mask first is where I separated from the pack. I'm not even going to hold you, it wasn't easy and I worked hard. I sacrificed things I wanted for the end game. I did, in fact, outwork the guys around me just like LP told me to do. So when my income jumped from $30k, while in training, to $54k, I was already accustomed to paying myself first. Out of habit, I banked no less than 20% of my pay and set it aside for emergency reserve savings, company stock purchases through payroll deduction and my 401(k) plan.

Two years into my new career, I decided that I had enough money saved to buy into a side hustle—rental real estate. I realized that wealth took more than just savings and I have always loved real estate so I took the plunge. I read in a novel many moons ago that people will always need a place to live and a place to die—both of which require land. I want to credit Toni Morrison for that but it may have been Alice Walker, Zora Neal Hurston or Maya Angelou who I also read a ton of. Land and bricks just made sense to me. I loved real estate because it was solid, as tangible as real money, and insurable against most risks.

At 24, I bought my first foreclosure property and then, two years later, I bought another rental property followed by another home that same year. What differentiated me from most side-hustle folks was that I had zero interest in quitting my job or touching the extra cash flow that I was getting from the rents. I used all the extra cashflow from my side hustle as a landlord to first build and maintain a six-month reserve of the property expenses and, once that account was funded, I used all the excess cashflow to pay down the mortgages faster.

What also differentiated me was that I didn't increase my lifestyle at the same rate as my income. By the time I hit six figures three years out of college, 70% of the guys I started with had already quit. I kept my head down and focused on hitting my net worth goal of $1 million by 30. To be clear, I'd like to take a moment to define net worth. I think I outlined it best in a tweet thread on November 23, 2019:

(1) Net worth is the most important calculation in personal finance. Your income and expenses are like quizzes and tests but your net worth is the report card—a culmination of what you've stacked based on what you're working with.

(2) Net worth is all of your assets minus all of your debts. Your assets are anything you own of value. Debt is an amount of money you borrowed from someone or an entity who intends to collect.

(3) Assets typically include: cash, stocks, bonds, mutual funds, buildings, land, trademarks and patents, appraised business valuation, valuable jewelry or artwork, vehicles, etc. (Note that income is not an asset)

(4) Liabilities typically include the outstanding balances (not monthly payments): credit cards, car loan, mortgages, home equity loan, personal loan, consolidation loan, student loan, the money borrowed from your loan shark auntie, etc.

Because net worth is defined by both assets and liabilities, it is virtually impossible to know how wealthy someone is without knowing both what they have and what they owe. Knowing someone has $800,000 of debt, for example, is not alone enough information to determine if they are in good shape financially because you need the other side of that equation—what assets are there to offset that debt. For my visual learners, if the person above had $300,000 in assets, they are in rough shape. Their net worth would be as follows:

Assets: $300,000

- Debts: $800,000

Net worth: -$500,000

If you formed an opinion of someone's wealth, on the basis of only knowing they had $800,000 in debt, you could be sorely mistaken if you didn't know their level of assets. For example, if someone has $800,000 in debt with $6,000,000 in assets, their net worth would be as follows:

Assets: $6,000,000

- Debts: $800,000

Net worth: $5,200,000

My ability to build my net worth quickly came from running on all cylinders simultaneously. My simple, yet effective, strategy was four parts:

• **Habit**: I started by saving no less than 20% of my income even when my pay was low. This became a force of habit.

• **Avoiding Lifestyle Inflation**: As my income increased, I kept my expenses low. Every victory or income increase didn't deserve a new car or bigger house. I invested what I didn't spend.

• **Side hustling**: I used savings to invest in real estate as a side hustle.

• **Snowflakes turn into Snowballs. Snowballs turn into avalanches**: I kept my job and reinvested 100% of the income (rent from properties and dividends from stocks) back into paying down debt and buying more assets. Reinvesting dividends and rental income exponentially compounded my returns and is arguably one of the cheapest and easiest ways to build wealth.

In our next Chapter, we will discuss maintaining different investment strategies for your short-, intermediate, and long-term goals and dive a little deeper into reinvesting income from your investments.

Step 6:

Keep some stash cash while investing and reinvesting your profits.

"One should have 3 buckets of money:

1. Short-term/emergency reserves – money you'll need in under 3 years.

2. Intermediate money – goals that are 3-7 years away.

3. Long term money – goals that are 7+ years out.

SPOILER ALERT: The 3 buckets shouldn't be invested the same way."

@ayeshaselden 12:48 PM ·1/3/2020 ·Twitter for iPhone

When you've successfully accomplished Steps 1 to 5, we are already beyond the space in your head that thinks it's impossible to stockpile a sufficient emergency fund and then invest the rest. We underestimate the simplistic ingenuity of maintaining 3 to 6 months of expenses in a low risk account (i. e. cash, money market, CDs). It's the basics we've heard a million times that we should do and still don't do.

Investors tend to forget the age-old tale that everything is for a season. There are periods of feast and periods of famine. The challenge with prolonged periods of feast, like the bull market that blessed investors for 11 years (March 9, 2009-March 11, 2020), is that we forget that famines always come. On November 11, 2019, exactly four months before the longest bull market in history ended, I tweeted:

"Landlords should have 6 months of total expenses in cash. If someone had 3 months cash + access to credit of 3 months, I wouldn't be mad. But no cash & 6 months of credit only is risky esp if you're mortgage heavy."

That wasn't an overly popular tweet but it certainly seemed to be prophetic. By April 2020, Chase bank, arguably the largest home lender in the country, stated that they are "temporarily pausing" accepting applications for home equity lines of credit. Other banks may follow suit. I wouldn't be surprised to see, like in 2008, banks announcing that they are closing existing lines of credit and/or converting existing balances into fixed installment loan products. If that available line was your only emergency reserve, that could be financially devastating.

The 2020 coronavirus pandemic caused a global shut down of large corporations and small businesses—triggering massive layoffs. And, as if it were an Aesop fable, the longest bull market in history was subsequently crushed by what would turn out to be the worst 1st quarter in history for the US stock market (Source: Fortune Magazine, March 31, 2020). Helluva an illustration of feast and famine.

On March 31, 2020, CNBC ran an article stating that Goldman Sachs is estimating upwards of 15% unemployment rates in the US. The Saint Louis Federal Reserve tossed out estimates that unemployment could hit 32%. Can you imagine roughly 1 in 3 Americans being out of work? It goes without saying that means many landlords won't be collecting rent and mortgages won't be getting paid.

We act broke and stack during periods of feast to better weather the famines. Homeowners/landlords with sufficient reserves are in a position of strength. Investors who are over-leveraged, and have low to no reserves, could be in a lot of trouble.

For clarity on reserves, the easiest way to calculate the amount you'll need is to tally all withdrawals, checks and debits from your bank statements and all credit card transactions for the last 3 months. You did this a few chapters ago in your recon mission. Except this time, you're not just highlighting your "wants"; you should be tallying **all** of your expenses for the last three months. That total is your baseline.

A more conservative approach would be to take that number and double it which puts you at 6 months of your total expenses in reserves. I like this method because it accounts for your fixed and discretionary expenses—which means you could maintain your lifestyle uninterrupted for at least 3 to 6 months. If your income was cut due to loss of a job, business or tenants, or The Rona, you could cut out some of the discretionary fluff in your budget based on your estimation of the longevity of that income-lull duration.

These funds should be maintained in an account that is liquid— meaning you can access the funds in under a week with little to no expense to you. They should be in an account that isn't connected to your regular checking account so you can't blow through the money easily. It should generally take a day or two before the funds can transfer to your regular account. That one to two day lag can be a cooling off period. A purchase that you may have thought you needed badly at the moment, may not seem as important 48 hours later.

Your emergency money should not be invested in things that could lose value. You should not be gambling these funds at the roulette table in the Showboat casino. This is your worst case scenario money. Not investing emergency reserves generally proves to be an almost impossible feat for investors. Investors almost always want to put their money to work and cash rates in today's markets are at historically low levels. Shooters are gonna shoot...but investors should always be mindful to separate their emergency cash from their long-term money.

A black swan event (look that up), like the 2008 recession and the coronavirus, is a great example of that worst case scenario. Let's assume you invested your emergency money in stocks right at the end of 2019, thinking you were clever and could earn a higher return on your cash than the banks were paying. You would have watched your "savings" money fall almost 35% between December 31 and March 23, 2020. Lets say you then got furloughed on March 24th. Welcome to risky assets. Risky assets require time. Emergencies are unforgivingly now based.

Cash above the 3-6 month of expenses should always be put to work in investment vehicles. How it is invested should be based on how soon the funds will be needed. Shorter time-frame goals should be invested less aggressively than funds you don't plan on touching for 7+ years. The goal is exponential growth and cash will not earn enough to multiply your money fast enough. I have

KEEP SOME STASH CASH WHILE INVESTING AND REINVESTING YOUR PROFITS.

long been an advocate of investing in dividend paying stocks and real estate because the income from both is like a silent partner adding to my wealth. Instead of using that income for my lifestyle now, however, I roll it right back into building more wealth.

If I have 1,000 shares of ABC stock and it pays me dividends of $3,000 per year, instead of blowing that $3,000 on wants, I use that dividend to buy 30 more shares of ABC stock. In the next year, I get paid a higher dividend because I'm now starting ahead of the game with 1,030 shares versus the 1,000 I had the year before. In the next year, my dividend would be more like $3,100 that I would use to reinvest—buying an additional 31 shares (assuming the share price remained flat).

The visual I get of how my reinvested dividends build wealth is imagining a small snowball on a mountaintop rolling downhill gathering more snow as the ball enlarges with each roll and collection. Left uninterrupted that snowball becomes as large as an avalanche. Reinvesting dividends and profits is getting wealthier with someone else's money. It is peak level investing.

Step 7:

When your passive income can afford the lifestyle you want FLEX ON EVERY MF WHO TOLD YOU IT WOULDN'T WORK.

"I sacrificed my 20s to build the foundation of long term wealth. I worked 60-80 hours/week, saved & invested. Folk said I would regret it. I'm 41 and can buy almost anything I want. Still waiting for that regret to kick in." @ayeshaselden 11:09 AM ·12/1/19 ·Twitter for iPhone

Man, I caught so much flack for this tweet from social media. I got everything from "where's her husband and kids?" (like the year was 1943) to "the only reason she's successful is because her mom is a college professor at an Ivy League school" (which she isn't). I even had one guy angrily comment on my Instagram page that it was **EVIDENT** I'd gotten a lucky financial windfall and that I couldn't have built my portfolios from scratch. My journey from the mud of The Passyunk Homes housing projects to owning millions in real estate, stocks and business ventures required a lot of work. As much as I hear folk say they love the mamba mentality, they also say they hate grind culture and tell those of us with strong work ethic things like "everything in balance". It's also apparent that many believe that only men can have the mamba mentality *insert a hard eye roll here*. As a

WHEN YOUR PASSIVE INCOME CAN AFFORD THE LIFESTYLE YOU WANT FLEX ON EVERY MF WHO TOLD YOU IT WOULDN'T WORK.

black woman, I constantly get told to stay humble while guys like Gary Vee get praised for the same message. I will also reserve my cheap shots for how imbalanced most people are in every area of their lives but not working too much is the hill they choose to die on.

The reality is that all of our paths are different and the key is to find the one that works for you. My strategy was to work hard early so that work was optional in my 40s. At 41, I could very comfortably retire today and never work another day in my life. That, to me, is balance.

What is not optional is ownership of assets that will provide you freedom and the life you've dreamt about. Quick story before I wrap. If you remember, I told you when I was in high school, I wanted to attend USC—although I had never in my life been to LA. My fascination with the city was entirely based on what I'd seen on TV and read in books. I arrived in LA for the very first time Memorial Day Weekend in 2002, at barely 24 years old, on a quick holiday vacation to celebrate the fact that I was about to purchase my first property back in Philly. My obsession with land and homes had already begun and, while the Hollywood section of LA looked nothing like the glamour I'd imagined, I fell in love with the city of angels. Before boarding my departing flight, I decided right then that I would do what it took to own property in LA, a sunny city where I could see mountains from my window and palm trees in the hood.

Over the years, I would buy and sell various investments and rehab dozens of homes in my hood back east. In 2018, I purchased and rehabbed a 4-unit building in a hood of North

Philly with cash from a flip I'd done the year prior. When I completed the renovations of the 4-unit property, I decided to dedicate that building to fulfilling the promise I made to my much younger self and bought a seven figure house in the View Park section of LA. The rents from that quadraplex in Philly pay the mortgage on my Los Angeles property each month. Wont He do it?

I'll leave you with this...there's absolutely nothing wrong with wanting nice things. What is wrong? Stunting too quickly. Flexing when you really shouldn't. Balling so hard when it should be a light dribble. Even though I have arrived at destination: financial independence, I **still** ask myself, "what assets will I acquire to pay for my luxuries?" That, my friends, is the ultimate flex.

Peace.